Protestant Dutch Church of the City of N.Y.

Commemoration of fifty years' service by the Rev. Thomas T.

Protestant Dutch Church of the City of N.Y.

Commemoration of fifty years' service by the Rev. Thomas T.

ISBN/EAN: 9783337274740

Printed in Europe, USA, Canada, Australia, Japan

Cover: Foto ©Lupo / pixelio.de

More available books at **www.hansebooks.com**

1839   1889

Commemoration

OF

Fifty Years' Service

BY

The Rev. Thomas E. Vermilye, D.D., LL.D.,

Senior Minister

OF

The Reformed Protestant Dutch Church

of the City of New York.

Published By Order of the Consistory

Prefatory Note.

AT a meeting of the Consistory held July 9, 1889, it was announced that the senior minister, the Rev. Dr. Vermilye, would complete in the autumn the fiftieth year of his connection with the Collegiate Church. As this was a period of continuous ministry which had been accomplished only once before in our history, it was determined to hold a commemorative service in the month of October, at which a proper expression of the views of the Consistory should be made, to be accompanied by similar words from representatives of the various bodies with which our senior minister had been associated. The Rev. Dr. Chambers and Messrs. Bookstaver, Locke and Brower were appointed a committee to make the necessary preparations, which they did after communicating with the recipient of the testimonial. The last Tuesday in the month was fixed for the time, and handsomely engraved cards of invitation were issued and widely distributed.

At a meeting of the Consistory held October 3d, a minute was adopted in reference to the event, which was engrossed in a peculiarly graceful form, attested by the signatures of the ministers, elders and deacons, and then bound in a style of simple but costly elegance. It was put in the hands of Dr. Vermilye on the evening of the commemoration.

There was a very large gathering at the Church, embracing some of the leading ministers of nearly every denomination and a great many prominent citizens, not a few of whom had been associated with Dr. Vermilye in different religious, charitable or literary institutions. The pulpit was occupied by the speakers of the occasion, and also the Hon. John Jay, the Hon. Seth Low, President-elect of Columbia College, Mr. John A. King, President of the New York Historical Society and the Rev. Dr. H. Y. Satterlee, while the members of the Great and Acting Consistories were seated in their usual pews on either side of the pulpit. One of our leading religious journals* in its graphic report of the jubilee thus spoke:

" The pulpit was tastefully decorated with palms and chrysanthemums, and on the communion table was a large frame-work of white chrysanthemums edged with maiden-hair ferns, and on this white background in red carnations were the dates 1839–1889. The service was most impressive throughout, and the care which had been bestowed by the committee of arrangements was rewarded in a service of dignity and beauty, which admirably befitted the occasion. The music was marked by rare taste, both in the appropriateness of the selections and their rendition. The united choirs of the Collegiate Churches sang well, and their part in the services was not marred by ostentatious display."

Besides the floral decorations in front of the pulpit there was on a stand near the desk a very beautiful basket of flowers, a voluntary offering from the Leake and Watts Orphan House.

---

* The New York *Observer.*

The Order of Exercises

BENEDIC ANIMA in B flat,   -   -   -   Dudley Buck

PRAISE the Lord, O my Soul,
> And all that is within me praise His holy name.
> Praise the Lord, O my Soul,
And forget not all His benefits.
Who forgiveth all thy sins,
> And healeth all thine infirmities.
Who saveth thy life from destruction,
> And crowneth thee with mercy and loving kindness.
O praise the Lord, ye angels of His,
> Ye that excel in strength.
Ye that fulfil His commandment,
> And hearken unto the voice of His word.
O praise the Lord, all ye His hosts,
> Ye servants of His that do His pleasure.
O speak good of the Lord, all ye works of His,
> In all places of His dominion.
Praise thou the Lord, O my Soul.

ADDRESS OF WELCOME, The Rev. Talbot W. Chambers, D.D., LL.D.

PRAYER, The Rev. James H. Mason Knox, D.D., LL.D., President of Lafayette College

THE RESOLUTIONS OF CONSISTORY AND ADDRESS, The Rev. Edward B. Coe, D.D.

THE RESPONSE, The Rev. Thomas E. Vermilye, D.D., LL.D.

HYMN: No. 557, " Glorious things of Thee are spoken."
("Austria,") F. J. Haydn

(TO BE SUNG STANDING)

GLORIOUS things of thee are
spoken,
Zion, city of our God ;
He whose word cannot be broken,
Formed thee for His own abode :
On the Rock of Ages founded,
What can shake thy sure repose ?
With salvation's wall surrounded,
Thou mayest smile at all thy
foes.

See, the streams of living waters,
Springing from eternal love,
Well supply thy sons and daugh-
ters,
And all fear of want remove :

Who can faint, while such a river
Ever flows their thirst to as-
suage ?
Grace, which, like the Lord, the
Giver,
Never fails from age to age.

Round each habitation hovering,
See the cloud and fire appear,
For a glory and a covering,
Showing that the Lord is near :
Thus deriving from their Banner
Light by night, and shade by day,
Safe they feed upon the manna
Which He gives them when
they pray.

ADDRESS, The Rev. Morgan Dix, S.T.D., Rector of Trinity
Church

ADDRESS, The Rev. Richard D. Harlan, Minister of the
First Presbyterian Church

MAGNIFICAT in A, - - - - - J. Stainer

MY soul doth magnify the Lord and my spirit hath rejoiced in
God my Saviour,
For He hath regarded the lowliness of His hand-maiden,
For behold, from henceforth all generations shall call me blessed,
For He that is mighty hath magnified me, and holy is His name,
And His mercy is on them that fear Him throughout all generations.
He hath showed strength with His arm,
He hath scattered the proud in the imagination of their hearts,
He hath put down the mighty from their seat and hath exalted the hum-
ble and meek.
He hath filled the hungry with good things,
And the rich He hath sent empty away.
He remembering his mercy hath holpen His servant Israel, as He prom-
ised to our forefathers
Abraham and his seed forever.

ADDRESS, The Hon. Enoch L. Fancher, President of the
American Bible Society

ADDRESS, Merrill E. Gates, LL.D., L.H.D., President of
   Rutgers College

DOXOLOGY

Praise God, from whom all blessings flow ;
Praise Him all creatures here below;
Praise Him above ye heavenly host ;
Praise Father, Son, and Holy Ghost.

BENEDICTION,   -   -   The Rev. Roderick Terry, D.D.

Committee

THE REV. TALBOT W. CHAMBERS, D.D., LL.D.
HON. HENRY W. BOOKSTAVER
FREDERICK T. LOCKE
WILLIAM L. BROWER

The United Choirs of the Collegiate Church

CARL WALTER, Organist of Church at Fifth Ave., and Forty-eighth St.
H. G. HANCHETT, Organist of Church at Fifth Ave., and Twenty-ninth St.
LOUIS C. JACOBY, Organist of Middle Church, Lafayette Place.

Commemorative Service

At eight o'clock the chair was taken by the Rev. Dr. Chambers, the Senior Acting Minister, and the Exercises commenced with the anthem Benedic Anima, Psalm CIII., in B flat, after which the chairman pronounced the short address of welcome that follows.

The Address of Welcome.

WE are gathered here, as the programme states, to commemorate the completion of fifty years of service by the senior minister of the Collegiate Church. That cycle of time is spoken of as most important. Mr. Gladstone told Mr. Depew last Summer that he considered it the most desirable half century in which any man could live. He referred to the progress which was made in Great Britain in the emancipation of the Roman Catholics, in the abolition of West India slavery, in the repeal of the corn laws, and in the removing the restrictions upon suffrage. Even so has it been upon the continent of Europe : witness the unification of Italy and of Germany ; the emancipation of the serfs in Russia ; the opening of China and Japan to commercial intercourse; the discovery of the sources of the Nile and the Congo, and the thorough exploration of inter-tropical Africa ; the accomplishment of the abolition of slavery throughout Christendom, for the last shackle has fallen from the last slave in a Christian land. Note, also, the extraordinary advances of physical science, much greater than in any previous century, and the flourishing literature of the Victorian period in every department of human genius. So, too, the progress in our own

country.   The annexation of Texas ; the war with Mexico ;
the acquisition of large territory on the Pacific ; the re-
moval of the Great American Desert which used to figure on
our maps, and the railroads crossing the continent ; the
marvellous development of the States on the Pacific slope ;
the war for the Union and its happy result ; the amazing
stimulus which it gave to every form of human effort.   All
these things make the half century distinct and memorable.

But our attention is turned from this wide outlook upon
public affairs to a single life: to fifty years in one man's
career.   Serving in the same church during all that period ;
in times of peace and in times of war ; meeting all the vi-
cissitudes of human things ; maintaining the same character
without shadow of change.

I remember very well dining with Dr. Vermilye in his
house at Albany in the month of July, 1839, and some
pleasantries were passed across the table respecting the
call which was then in contemplation.   During the whole
intervening period he has been able to hold steadfast his
position, and to discharge all the various duties which come
upon a minister in a metropolitan church, besides those belonging strictly to his own parish.

In the name of the Consistory it is my pleasure and
province to thank you for your presence, to welcome you
here, and invite you to join with us in giving proper attention and emphasis to a career so distinguished.   Many of
those who were invited accepted the invitation and are
present.   Others have declined with regret, among whom I
may mention his honor, Hugh J. Grant, Mayor ; Justices
Bradley and Blatchford of the Supreme Court of the United
States ; Rev. Noah Porter, D.D., LL.D., ex-President of
Yale University ; Rev. Josiah Strong, Secretary of the
Evangelical Alliance ; Alex. E. Orr, President of the New
York Produce Exchange ; The Rev. Drs. Mabon, Wood-
bridge and Demarest of the Theological Seminary at New
Brunswick, N. J.; Right Rev. Henry C. Potter, D.D.,
LL.D., Bishop of the Diocese ; Right Rev. Bishop Bedell ;
Rev. John W. Brown, D.D. ; Rev. Wm. J. Seabury, D.D. ;

Rev. Henry Mottet, D.D.; Rev. Cornelius B. Smith, D.D.; Rev. Philip A. H. Brown; Rev. Wm. T. Sabine, D.D.; Rev. Geo. D. Boardman, D.D., of Philadelphia; Rev. J. S. Riggs, D.D., of Auburn; Rev. J. M. Stevenson, D.D.; Rev. Howard Crosby, D.D.; Rev. J. M. Worrall, D.D.; Rev. S. B. Rossiter, D.D.; Rev. Wm. M. Taylor, D.D.; Rev. Geo. H. Smyth, D.D.; Rev. David Waters, D.D., of Newark, N. J.; Rev. Herman C. Berg, of Brooklyn; Rev. Livingston L. Taylor, of Port Jervis, N. Y.; Rev. F. N. Zabriskie, D.D., of Princeton, N. J.; Rev. R. S. MacArthur, D.D.; Rev. Robert Collyer; Rev. J. D. Wickham, an uncle of a former mayor of this City, who in his ninety-third year is still vigorous in mind and body; Stephen P. Nash, Esq.; Prof. Geo. L. Peabody; Hon. Robert B. Roosevelt; Wm. H. Crosby; Hon. Abraham Lansing, Albany; A. L. Ackerman, Titusville, Pa.; Ten Eyck Sutphen, of Brooklyn; Chas. H. Booth, of Englewood, N. J.; Peter R. Warner; Allan C. Hutton, of New Brunswick, N. J.

It is proper on every such occasion to invoke the divine presence and blessing, and this will now be done for us by the Rev. James H. Mason Knox, D.D., LL.D., President of Lafayette College, the son of the eminent man who was the senior minister of this church when Dr. Vermilye was called.

Prayer.

ALMIGHTY and ever blessed God, Father, Son and Holy Ghost, lift up upon us thy countenance and give us peace.

We come into Thy presence with grateful praise. We give Thee most hearty thanks for the circumstances of goodness and loving kindness in which we are assembled this night in the Sanctuary of Thy house.

We remember the days of old, and bless Thy name that in many generations Thou hast led this people like a flock by the hand of men whom Thou hast counted faithful putting them into the ministry, and who approved themselves as the ministers of God, by pureness, by knowledge, by long suffering, by kindness, by the Holy Ghost, by love unfeigned, by the Word of truth, by the power of God : who watched for souls as they who must give account, that they might do it with joy and not with grief.

O Lord God of Israel, there is no God like Thee in Heaven above or in Earth beneath, who keepest covenant and mercy with Thy servants.

We lift up our hearts and voices to Thee to-night in humble adoration and praise for what our ears have heard, and our eyes have seen, and our souls have felt of Thy great goodness to this congregation called by Thy name by the men whom Thou hast given to it as Thy ambassadors to declare Thy will. We thank Thee for the grace of which they have been the almoners, for the light and peace and comfort of Thy word, which they ministered by the Holy Ghost sent down from heaven, and for the help they gave to whatsoever hastened the day when He who was delivered for our offences and raised for our justification shall come again without sin unto salvation.

And, now, gracious God, God and Father of our Lord and Saviour Jesus Christ, we thank Thee for Thy servant, our venerated father, whose long continuance in the pastorate of this church we celebrate to-night ; for his work and labor of love in the care of souls, for his rightly divining the Word of truth, for his manifestation of the Spirit of Him who came to seek that which was lost, for his gentleness, aptness to teach, and patience.

We bless Thee that in all things he has made full proof of his ministry received of the Lord Jesus, and that now that he wears the hoary head as a crown of glory because found in the way of righteousness, his eye is not dim nor his natural force abated.

Thou art faithful, O our God, to Thy word ; they that be planted in the house of the Lord shall flourish in the courts of our God. They shall still bring forth fruit in old age to show that the Lord is upright. He is our Rock and there is no unrighteousness in Him.

With tender love we commend our father to Thy most holy keeping, for what remains to him of this mortal life. Thou hast been his shepherd, and he has not wanted any good thing. Thou hast made him to lie down in green pastures. Thou hast led him beside the still waters. Thou hast anointed his head with oil. His cup runneth over. Surely goodness and mercy have followed him all the days of his life, and he shall dwell in the house of the Lord forever. He has fought a good fight, he has kept the faith, and there is laid up for him a crown of righteousness which the Lord shall give him in that day.

Till that hour of his coronation, we entreat Thee, good Lord, deal very gently with him. Smooth his pathway. Sustain his faltering steps. Give him abundance of Thy peace, and when the last of earth shall come, give him to fall asleep in Jesus to awake in the blessedness of those who have turned many to righteousness, and who shall shine as the stars forever and ever.

And we entreat thy favor, Almighty God, still to abide with this church, this branch so manifestly of thy planting, that Thou mayest be glorified. In the years that are past, Thou hast been with it to make it a power in the earth for the praise of Thy name. At this time when it is engaged in these acts of piety, gratitude and love, on which Thou lookest so approvingly, be pleased, O Lord most merciful, to show thyself in the outpouring of Thy good Spirit on all who are here and all who are represented here.

Arise, O Lord, into Thy rest, Thou and the ark of Thy Strength. Let Thy priests be clothed with righteousness and let Thy saints shout for joy. Here do Thou dwell. Abundantly bless the provision of Thy house. Satisfy Thy poor with bread.

And so we pray for the Church universal. Grace, mercy and peace from God our Father, and the Lord Jesus Christ be with it. Hasten the day, Lord God of Israel, the blessed promised day when the watchmen on the walls of Zion shall lift up the voice. With the voice together shall they

sing, for they shall see eye to eye, for the Lord has brought
again Zion.

All we ask in His name, and for His sake who has taught
us when we pray to say:

OUR FATHER WHICH ART IN HEAVEN, HALLOWED BE
THY NAME, THY KINGDOM COME, THY WILL BE DONE IN
EARTH AS IT IS IN HEAVEN, GIVE US THIS DAY OUR
DAILY BREAD, AND FORGIVE US OUR TRESPASSES AS WE
FORGIVE THOSE WHO TRESPASS AGAINST US, LEAD US
NOT INTO TEMPTATION, BUT DELIVER US FROM EVIL,
FOR THINE IS THE KINGDOM, THE POWER AND THE
GLORY FOR EVER, AMEN.

The Chairman then said: An appropriate minute in reference to the
fifty years of service of Dr. Vermilye, has been prepared by the Consistory. This will now be read in your hearing by the Rev. Dr.
Coe, who will accompany it with an address to which Dr. Vermilye
himself will respond.

The Resolutions of Consistory.

THE minute adopted by the Consistory of this church
at their last regular meeting is as follows :

"REFORMED PROTESTANT DUTCH CHURCH
OF THE CITY OF NEW YORK.
In Consistory, October 3, 1889

1. As the Reverend Thomas Edward Vermilye, D.D.,
LL.D., will conclude during the present month the fiftieth
year of his service as one of the Ministers of the Collegiate
Church, the Consistory have much pleasure in expressing as
follows their sentiments on the interesting occasion.

2. We devoutly recognize the goodness of our Heavenly Father in preserving the life and health of our senior
pastor, so that he has accomplished a longer term of service
than any of his predecessors save only the Rev. Gualterus
DuBois, whose ministry began in the year 1699 and ended
with his life in the year 1751.

3. During this long tract of years, so eminent in science and letters as to be known as the brilliant Victorian period, Dr. Vermilye was enabled to fulfill the functions of his office, both as preacher and pastor, with signal ability and success.

4. Being contemporary with eight colleagues, three of whom, the revered Knox, Brownlee and DeWitt, have gone to their reward, he with them has habitually maintained the dignity and usefulness of our metropolitan pulpit, and showed himself a workman that needeth not to be ashamed.

5. In the various public institutions with which he was connected, whether belonging to our own denomination or the church in general, he was fitted to render, and did render, most efficient service as a wise counsellor, a faithful officer, and an eloquent advocate.

6. Having been born and brought up in this City where he commenced his ministry in the year 1826, though afterwards he prosecuted it for a time in West Springfield, Mass., and again in Albany, and having spent a half-century in subsequent labor here, he became completely identified with its interests, and was always active and zealous in forwarding whatever contributed to its welfare.

7. In his private and domestic life, and in intercourse with his brethren of all branches of the church catholic, he strikingly illustrated the virtues to be expected from his Huguenot descent and his representative connection with an ancient church of Holland origin.

8. Although his life-time is almost contemporaneous with the century now approaching its tenth decade of years, we trust that the same gracious Providence which has preserved hitherto the fulness of his mental vigor and so large a measure of bodily strength, will continue the same gifts for years to come.

9. In view of all the foregoing the Consistory now appoint the 29th day of the present month for a public service to be held in the church on Fifth Avenue and Forty-eighth Street, at which this minute shall be read, and appropriate addresses made by representatives of sister churches."

DR. COE: I have now the honor and pleasure of handing a suitably engrossed copy of this minute to the Rev. Dr. Vermilye.   .

The Address of the Rev. Dr. Coe.

THE pleasant duty which has been entrusted to me this evening of adding to the resolutions just read a few personal words, might perhaps have been more appropriately committed to my senior colleague, Dr. Chambers. For my personal acquaintance with the Collegiate Church and its ministers does not go back very far. It covers only the last ten years. Of the beginning of Dr. Vermilye's ministry in this City I cannot speak from my own personal knowledge, since I was at that time literally less than the least of these my brethren, for I was not even born. And yet these last ten years of delightful intercourse and association with the dear and venerable gentleman whose jubilee we are met to celebrate to-night, have been like a perfect afternoon in Summer, which in its tranquil and satisfying beauty shows plainly enough what the early morning must have been, and what the high and brilliant noon.

It is to all of us, who are variously related to this church, a matter of sincere rejoicing and of devout gratitude to God, that He has permitted us to see this day. A half century is a long time, longer than the majority of human lives, much longer than the active career even of most of those who are spared to a good old age. And yet in the history of this country it would be possible to gather together not a few names (and it would be a catalogue of noble and illustrious names) of men who have passed a half century of years in the active and efficient ministry of the gospel, holding to the last the same inspiring faith which animated them at the beginning, and proclaiming it with that broadening charity and that deepening tenderness and sympathy which are the beautiful fruit of a long experience of life. But a ministry of this length in *one* church is very rare. It is in our days extremely infrequent. It was not common even in the more sedate and slow-moving days of our fathers. The Dutch Church enjoys an excellent reputation for keeping its ministers and for taking good care of them, but of the thirty men who have held the office of minister of the Collegiate Church since it was organized in July, 1628, only *one* has until now occupied the position for fifty years—Domine Du Bois, who came to this country from Holland in 1699 and who died in 1751. Of the others *seven* have been in the service of this church for forty years or more, including three of the colleagues of Dr. Vermilye, Dr. Knox, Dr. DeWitt and our honored and beloved Dr. Chambers. And it is interesting to observe how few such careers, succeeding one another, are needed to carry us back to a time which seems very remote. Six years before Dr. Vermilye was installed in the old Middle Church on Nassau street, Dr. Gerardus Kuypers died. But Dr. Kuypers was himself installed on the Sunday following the day on which General Washington was inaugurated President of the United States. Thus the ministries of these two men, with a gap of only six years between them, cover the whole century of our history as an independent and self-governing nation. In 1789 Domine Ritzema was still living, having been summoned from Holland in 1744 as a colleague of Du Bois, who was born in 1666. It is thus easy to believe that the elder of these two men must often have rehearsed to his younger associate his recollections of those stirring times, distant from us by two centuries, when the great revolution in England ended in the accession of the Dutch stadtholder to the throne, and the liberties of both countries were finally secured by the third William of Orange. Measured in this way, how short time seems! And how many momentous events may be covered by a single human life!

But it belongs to Dr. Vermilye rather than to me to speak of the changes that he has witnessed. I am rather to say a word of that which has *not* changed in all these fifty years—the feeling of respect and confidence and affection which all who have here been associated with him have cherished towards him.   Many of them are not here to give utterance to it.   Of those who welcomed him at his coming, but few remain; most of them are fallen asleep.   Of his eight colleagues *three*, whose names are still honored in all this community, Knox, Brownlee and DeWitt, have gone up to receive the reward of their long and eminent service.   The composition of the consistory and the membership of the church have almost completely changed as the years have gone forward.   Instead of the fathers have come the children, and the children's children, and many who were not "to the manner born" have found in this ancient church their Christian home.   But we who are now here are at one with those who have left us in our loving regard for him whose completed half century of labor we celebrate tonight.   If we do not ourselves remember it, we know very well with what grace and beauty of person and manner, with what charming melody and fervor of speech, with what strength of Christian conviction, and what fire of Christian enthusiasm he came to his work in this city fifty years ago. We know with what fidelity and persuasiveness and power he has preached the unsearchable riches of Christ, year after year and decade after decade, to great congregations who came to love and honor *him*, while he taught them to love and honor the Master.   We know with what unfailing courtesy and tact, with what tenderness of sympathy and wisdom of counsel he has mingled with those who have always welcomed his presence in their homes as at once their pastor and their friend.   Many now present will recall the lofty and animated eloquence with which he maintained the cause of truth and righteousness and national honor in the trying days of the Civil War.   And a much larger number of persons than this church could hold are conscious of their indebtedness to him for religious instruction, consolation and incentive, while they have felt that the consistent beauty of his Christian life was an alluring illustration of the gospel that he preached.   It has been an honor and an advantage to the church of which he has now for many years been the

Senior Pastor, that he has held so high a social position in this community and has been able and ready to serve in the administration of so many important institutions of philanthropy and of religion, some of which are represented here this evening, to add their tribute of respect and gratitude to ours. It is a noble and useful career over which he can now look back, with nothing in it to be ashamed of or concealed ; and we all—his colleagues in this ministry, the officers and members of this church, and those who are more or less closely associated with us—have felt the unanimous and hearty desire to mark the fiftieth anniversary of his installation by this service of public recognition and regard. We congratulate him upon that which is past,—upon the work that he has done, upon the well merited honors that he has already received. We rejoice that he is with us still. We pray that, if the Master will, he may yet tarry with us for many years. If we see and hear him less frequently now than a few years ago in our pulpits, we love to see him in our social gatherings, at our Sabbath worship, in our homes and in his own. Whenever we are called to bid farewell to those whom God takes from us, we feel that his words of consolation and hope have a meaning and a power which the words of younger men do not possess. And at the Lord's Table we love to see him; his presence there is itself a benediction. To me at least the Holy Sacrament, as often as we observe it, seems to lack something if, before we rise, we do not hear his voice, growing more tender and more impressive every year, speaking to us of the love of the dear Lord, whom he has served so long, and who is then so near to him and to us all. At such times I have often thought, as many others, no doubt, have also thought, of the familiar story of the Apostle John, that in his old age, when his active ministry was ended, he used still to meet at times with the church at Ephesus, and with the light of the Master's glory shining on his face, to say to those who were gathered around him, " Little children, love one another."

Dear friend and father, may God keep you in His love,

and fulfill to you the promise that at evening time there shall be light—within, around, and above !

The Response by the Rev. Dr. Vermilye.

I SHOULD be strangely lacking in sensibility, hardly fit to be called human, if I could appear in this place on this occasion, without profound emotion. You assemble to offer your congratulations on the close of a pastorate of fifty years. First, my grateful acknowledgments I humbly offer to the Angel of the Covenant that has led me and fed me all my life long. Nor can I, nor would I refrain from returning to the Consistory, the people of the congregation, and to you revered brethren and friends, my heartfelt thanks for this memorable token of kind regard.

I feel that I have come to a very solemn point in my life's history. The current of thought turns back, not through half a century of years only in this church, but almost to the hour of my earliest consciousness in this my native city;—then of small limits, now arraying itself in grandeur, spreading onward and outward, and destined, as it seems, to become the metropolis of the world. The past is again present. Objects then familiar, but now obliterated; forms and faces of relatives and friends long since gone, seem to present themselves as living realities; echoes rise from the deep solitude of bygone days; voices seem to come up all around me, saying in tones of solemn admonition "The place whereon thou standest is holy ground." The years have been very swift—startling in the number they have so noiselessly multiplied—and age has come, apt to be burdened with bodily infirmities, to feel abatement of mental vigor, reverses and bereavements, premonitions of final departure. Yet is it not always nor necessarily dark and joyless. Often "at eventide it is light." A Christian spirit softened by time and grace may learn to bow with sweet submission to a Father's will; leans lovingly on Jesus' bosom; stretches out the wings of faith and hope, essaying to rise to better regions and a holier communion. And thus even the hoary head may become a crown of glory.

At the time when I came to the Collegiate Church in 1839 the Old Middle, an antique structure, afterwards the United States Post Office, on Cedar, Nassau, and Liberty streets; the North, a fine edifice on the corner of Fulton and William Streets; and the new granite church at the corner of Fourth Street and Lafayette Place, were the places of worship. The Consistory Building was at the corner of Nassau and Ann Streets. A large portion of the people lived below Chambers Street and the down town churches had yet large congregations, but the flow had commenced up town which made the new church and another minister necessary when I was called to the co-pastorate. It is a singular historical memory that when it was proposed to build on Lafayette Place the project was met in the Consistory with strenuous opposition, it being said that a congregation could never be gathered in that far-off region. The same thing was true, as I had good reason to know, when the Twenty-ninth Street, and in a measure, when the Forty-eighth Street church was built. So little did old New Yorkers realize the prospective growth of our city and the necessity of church extension. But indeed, what prophetic eye could have foreseen the vast proportions it has attained in fifty years, or the still greater it shall attain in the fifty years to come. At once, however, the new Fourth Street church was filled, and soon it was found necessary to open a small edifice on Ninth Street, between Broadway and the Bowery, as a chapel of ease.

The Pastors in 1839 were the Rev. Drs. Knox, Brownlee, and De Witt; very diverse in their gifts, but all able and faithful men. After Dr. Brownlee was laid aside by paralysis, the Rev. Dr. Chambers was called, and subsequently the Rev. Drs. Joseph T. Duryea, James M. Ludlow, and William Ormiston have held the pastorate but have retired to other spheres of labor. I was the last minister installed

in the venerable Old Middle church. And it is worthy of
remark that the church edifices existing when I became
pastor have all disappeared before the advance of trade.
The ancient order of rotation in ministerial services has also
given place within the last twenty years to separate pastorates, the option having been reserved to me of preaching in
the churches in rotation on Sabbath mornings.

A pastorate of fifty years in the same church, to which
may be added in my case pleasant and I hope not unprofit-
able ministries in Vandewater Street in this city; in West
Springfield, Mass., and in the ancient Dutch church in Albany, making about sixty-three years of ministerial service;
—such a pastorate although unusual in these days of mi-
gratory pastorates, in general must present much uniform-
ity with little to gratify curiosity. Yet the pastor's diary,
prepared in a right spirit, might be very instructive. Ministers are often brought into the inmost scenes of individual
and domestic life; into connection with strange and sometimes beautiful developments of character; with exciting
experiences religious and irreligious; with the doubts and
the ecstacies, the hopes and the dreads which agitate the
human heart. And to be made, in a sense, the physician of
souls is an awful trust. Surely he should aim to be refined
in feeling, gentle in speech, not brusque nor rough in manners, and earnest in piety. Of his public functions in an established charge, pastoral visitation is prominent; mainly
valuable, however, as it must be, conducted in a city like
this, in bringing pastor and people into kindly acquaintance
and so preparing them for mutual benefit; him to know
their state and wants, them to receive his message with
profit.

With the great increase of population, also, within half a
century great changes have taken place in the line of Christian work. It is a day of action. Benevolent societies are
to be conducted both in and out of the church; the poor to
be looked after tenderly, visited and ministered unto, and a
Christian sagacity used with rich and poor to " compel them
to come in." The larger part of these manifold agencies

has grown up within fifty years, and all rely upon the pastor for sympathy and active co-operation.

But the great work of the pastor is to be a teacher "holding forth the word of life." Go, preach the gospel, teaching all nations, is His divine commission. " Preach the word," saith Paul. "I am set," saith he "for the defence of the gospel." By this must be meant a definite system of truth, entirely distinct from the prevailing philosophies and religions. It is styled "the faith"; things to be believed. The church of God has ever had its fixed faith. It has ever maintained that "holy men of God spake as they were moved by the Holy Ghost." What they gave forth was therefore, in the strictest sense, God's word. They were instructed what to say and how to say it. The scriptures indited by them were divinely inspired and therefore of absolute authority, all-sufficient for life and doctrine. Less than infallible in the whole and in its parts, it ceases to be God's word. The specific teachings of these scriptures have from time to time been formulated into convenient creeds, such as the so-called Apostles' Creed, and the creeds of the Reformed Churches; the Heidelberg Catechism, the Thirty-nine Articles of the Protestant Episcopal Church, the Westminster Catechism and Confession, and other Reformed symbols. These all contain one system; speak substantially one language; embody the cardinal principles of the New Testament, and thus express "the faith delivered to the saints." Upon the doctrines thus set forth the life of the Church has hung in all ages; on them its influence and glory depend. As they are kept in the popular mind and affirmed or weakened by the ministry, has the Church put on her beautiful garments, or walked in sackcloth and depression. Moreover it should be particularly noted that these consentient creeds, formed at different times, in different countries, by men of very diverse culture, must be taken as so many independent testimonies to the divine nature of the communications and of the doctrines which the Bible certainly teaches. The least that can be affirmed is that all these learned and devout men in conscientious search of truth, in such varying conditions, have ever found the Bible to be such as their creeds declare. Yet this faith of the Church has been received with no easy credulity, but in all times has encountered the keenest examination and the most hostile criticism. Nor this from the ignorant nor profane alone, but notably from science and learning without, and from speculation within its own bosom.

I have lately re-read Mosheim's Ecclesiastical History, valuable for its arrangement and statement of facts and opinions, and particularly useful for its chapters on the heresies and divisions in each century. Never has the faith seemed at rest. No learning or ingenuity, no objection that imagination could invent to modify or overthrow the word and its doctrines, has been wanting; objectors have reviled; sects have arisen; but here it stands stable as the pillared firmament. The Ark has outridden every storm. Amidst the precious relics of the ancient world, the wealth of poetry, eloquence, art, no gift so precious as our Bible has come down the stream of time. Paul met the " oppositions of science falsely so-called," but before the simple word preached, the subtleties of the Greek philosophies faded away and believers were multiplied. No learning or sagacity of modern times have excelled the attacks of Porphyry and Celsus, but they have been long forgotten, while the Bible and the old faith of our creeds lives on and spreads. Who now reads the deistical writers of the last century, able beyond example as they were and determined to banish the blessed Gospel from the earth. But the word of the Lord endureth. Nor was it ever more manifest than at this hour that it has within it "the power of an endless life." The impelling motive of most of these opponents is pride of intellect or hatred of what to us appears to be as much a dictate of reason as a doctrine of revelation, to wit, that the Supreme Ruler must be held "to do his pleasure in the armies of heaven and among the inhabitants of the earth." That by a wonderful combination "justice and judgment are the habitation of his throne, while mercy and truth go before his face." Hence the awful doctrine of absolute sovereignty, wherever it appears, is resented in seeming forgetfulness that there are awful facts in God's daily providence which are seen and felt, and can be neither disputed nor resisted. The secret spirit of much objection and of some sects, is undoubtedly a wish to modify or exclude this principle in its far-reaching relations. Yet glorious sovereignty and boundless love go hand in hand in the government of the world, and in the scheme of gospel truth.

The last fifty years, and indeed the last century, have been marked with uncommon mental activity and boldness in various departments of learning. New discoveries in science as is claimed, and new theories have as usual been brought into sharp antagonism with the Bible and the truths which shine on its pages as if written with a sunbeam. Perhaps the most formidable attack upon our faith ever made from this quarter is now in progress. But the bearing of the alleged facts and their relations to revealed truth are yet under discussion, and in the contest unbelief may not yet exult. When we consider the past history of mental and even of physical science : the limits of human reason ; the natural ardor and positiveness of inventors and discoverers how often what was yesterday received as demonstration is modified or rejected to-day ; and how apparently irreconcilable diversities have by fuller knowledge been harmonized ; modesty and reserve are seen to be a prime requirement in all human investigations. Nor do we doubt, since all truth is one, that what is proved true in the claims of modern science will in the end be found in full accord with the principles the Christian Church has always gathered from Holy Writ. The consonance of its doctrines with the wants of the soul, and its entire history, forbid us to fear.

Within the Church, also, various imagined improvements have appeared. Of this class are the Future Probation theory and the Higher Criticism. These are not new. For a large part they are pure speculation ; and a logical mind will perceive that they are on lines of thought which, if

severely pursued, will lead into most objectionable posi-
tions;—the former into Universalism, and the latter even
into simple Deism.

Another insidious opponent to the received faith of the
Church, and a boasted substitute for it, appears in a popular humanitarianism. Law and sin; ruin in Adam and
recovery only by the atonement of Jesus the crucified; the
soul-renewing Spirit and the eternal Judgment are themes
little regarded;—indeed, in reality disrelished. And Paul's
expositions of the Christian verities are unsavory. Man
and his relations to this life are mainly considered ; the vir-
tuous play of the amiable instincts of nature and personal
well-being here, will be a sure passport to a divine reward
hereafter. This scheme can hardly be said to have been
congested into a system or a separate sect, but is diffused
through several, where it finds a congenial home. And yet
mere philanthropy, though admirable in its sphere, is in no
proper sense a religion,—a binding the soul back to God.
In truth, if it rise not from the sure foundation Jesus Christ,
it is little better than disguised paganism. And pagan
morality, however refined, however exquisitely set forth in
forms of beautiful speech, never had the power to curb and
purge the wild passions of the soul or to renovate the
domestic and social conditions, and was a failure even for
this world. Seneca's morals, written amidst the highest re-
finements of the highest classes in imperial Rome, but in
the most corrupt state of society the civilized world probably ever saw, had no influence upon his age, scarcely upon
himself. Man is immortal! Man is accountable! And no
scheme of mere moral teaching has ever yet had power to
invigorate conscience to its awful functions and steady the
faltering footsteps of earth's wayward pilgrims, or answer
the fearful question " Wherewith shall I come before the
Lord." The blood of Christ alone can give light, peace,
assurance, " the joy unspeakable and full of glory." Not
human virtue but a divine daysman must be its strength.
And this modern philanthropy for religion, without conviction of sin, without spiritual conversion, without an atoning

Saviour, is as cold and deathlike as the vicinage of the grave.

These are some of the existing issues and thus throughout her history the Church and her faith, according to prediction, have been in constant conflict yet evermore victorious. Her ministry still proclaims those pregnant truths which have ever given peace and hope to men; which gave new life to the world amidst the ruins of falling empire and an effete idolatry; and her bow still abides in strength. We have heard much of " Progressive Christianity " and the " Church of the future." That there may be variations of form, and that there will be a fresh outpouring of the Spirit, is to be expected. But if it is intended that men shall ever get beyond the Bible or its peculiar doctrines as summarized in our catechisms and creeds; shall reach something higher, holier, more sublime ;—it is a pretense fraudulent and delusive. These truths were given not for a race or an age, but for all times and all people. Their message is to man; the same to the Jew and the Gentile, the learned and the savage. The old teachings contained within the covers of our Bible and the ordinances of the New Testament Church are sufficient and perpetual.

The earth moves, indeed ; it is in one constant flow, but there are things upon it that never change. The grand Pyramid has loomed upon the desert for ages past and will continue until the final consummation. So the Church which is the pillar and ground of the truth is monumental and imperishable. The sacred Book it is commissioned to guard and diffuse to all nations; its ministry which has lived in succession hitherto and with which the Saviour has promised to abide until the end of the world ; its appointed ordinances ;—these shall never be lost and can never change. They are God's ordained means to gather his elect from the ruins of the fall, and they will stand while there is a sinner to be saved by grace or a saint to be sanctified and speeded on his way; while the earth remaineth and until the light that burns in yonder sky goes out and ancient darkness comes again. Nor then shall his glorious Gospel have

failed. But the Church in the wilderness shall pass to the
Church of the first-born in heaven; and to the redeemed
throng of "numbers without number," justified in the name
of the Lord Jesus and by the Spirit of our God, shall be
thrown wide the celestial gates "on golden hinges turning."
These will be the trophies of divine wisdom and power and
love for which the earth was upreared and rolled out its
ages; in which the great problems of moral agency and
predetermination, of providence, of sin, and of redemption,
were wrought out and forever solved, and sovereign wisdom and love have triumphed. " And the ransomed of the
Lord shall return and come to Zion with songs and everlasting joy upon their heads; they shall obtain joy and
gladness, and sorrow and sighing shall flee away."

That we may all come to that blissful re-union is the
Pastor's fervent prayer.

At the conclusion of Dr. Vermilye's remarks all joined in the singing
of Hymn No, 557, " Glorious things of Thee are Spoken, "
(" Austria ") J. F. Haydn.

After which the chairman said :—" When the Rev. Dr. MORGAN DIX was
invited to be present and speak on this occasion, he consented in a
very cordial and graceful letter. The reason why he is not here
will appear by the following letter, which I will read :— "

TRINITY RECTORY, October 29th, 1889.

" DEAR DR. CHAMBERS :—I regret very sincerely that I
cannot be with you this evening, but I am suffering from a
heavy cold, and my physician forbids me to go out at
night.

" When you invited me to the Commemorative Service
about to be held, you asked me to say a few words on the
occasion. If I had been present I should have complied
literally with your request ; as it is, I shall write what I intended to say.

" It gives me great pleasure to add my voice to those
which now do honour to the venerable and eminent Senior
Minister of the Reformed Protestant Dutch Church in the
City of New York. Dr. Vermilye and I have been for

nearly thirty years co-workers in the Board of Trustees of the Leake and Watts Orphan House. It is one of those Boards, which are composed of ex-officio members, and it has the happy effect of bringing together clergymen who otherwise might not have had an opportunity of working side by side. As a member of these Boards, I have had the advantage of knowing many eminent men; Dr. Phillips, of the First Presbyterian Church, Dr. Paxton, his successor, and my young friend and brother, Mr. Harlan. Thus also I became intimately acquainted with that most excellent man, the Rev. Dr. De Witt, whom to know was to love; and thus were Dr. Vermilye and I brought together.

"I have observed him attentively for many years, and have come to respect, to honour, to admire, and to hold him in affectionate regard. He seems to me to fill the measure of a good man ; a simple-hearted and sincere Christian, always deeply interested in his work ; ever courteous and refined ; bright, cheerful, cordial, scholarly, able in speech, adorning his conspicuous position. His interest in the little orphan children has been constant and touching, as became a faithful guardian of their interests.

"It gives me pleasure to think how often he has expressed his admiration for that branch of the church to which I belong. Again and again have I seen him in my parish church on Ascension Day ; indeed we used to look for him there as a matter of course. You may, perhaps, remember what the good Doctor said at the Quarter-Millennial Anniversary in 1878. He praised us highly ; but went on to add, with a certain quiet humor, that, in his opinion, the reason why the Episcopal Church is so flourishing and prosperous, is this ; that it has absorbed so many of the Dutch Reformed communion. Let me retort on my friend, and add that, if we had known each other earlier, and if he had been then in his present favorable disposition toward us, I should have endeavoured to persuade him to follow a good example and to reinforce and aid us still further in his own person.

"But I do not grudge you this great ornament of your

body ; on the contrary, I congratulate you on the lustre which he has cast on you, and on the honour which has come to you from that admirable character, that spotless name, and the record of half a century of true and laudable service now happily complete.

"As for himself, I have only this to add. The time is short, the hour cannot be far distant at which the earthly tie must be broken, and he shall see man no more with the inhabitants of the world. Let not this be called a falling of the shadows, an oncoming of nocturnal stillness. Nay, but these last days of the earthly life of our venerabie and beloved friend are the beginning of the dawn, the approach of the day. For him it is the night which is far spent, the day which is at hand. For him the skies are brightening with the approach of the morning of the Kingdom of Heaven. God bless him and keep him, and make him to be numbered with the saints in glory everlasting! And may we be strengthened by his example, and, like him, be enabled to stand firm in our lot to the end of the days and to finish our course with joy. I remain, My dear Doctor,

"Very truly yours,

"MORGAN DIX."

To this may be added a letter from the Right Reverend HENRY C. POTTER, who, in like manner, had courteously and with a great manifestation of interest, welcomed the invitation which was given him to attend.

"DIOCESAN HOUSE, 29 Lafayette Place.

"NEW YORK, Oct. 28th, 1889.

"MY DEAR DR. CHAMBERS:—When I wrote you last, I saw no obstacle that I could not remove, to my presence with you to-morrow evening. But an imperative engagement, which I cannot postpone, takes me out of town, and thus deprives me of what would have been a very great pleasure.

"It is my honorable privilege to serve with Dr. Vermilye, as his junior, in the joint Chaplaincy of the St. Nicholas Society, and it has been my pride for many years to reckon him as among my most dear and honored friends, as he was that of my venerable predecessor in the Episcopate of this Diocese. I well remember when St. Thomas Church. was opened, seeing Dr. Vermilye advance to the Chancel rail to receive the Holy Communion, and no one who recalls that scene will forget the tender eagerness with which the late Bishop of New York at once came forward to claim for himself the privilege of administering to his cherished and lifelong friend. My own friendship is thus a sacred inheritance. All honor to him, " *Clarum et venerabile nomen*," whom all who know and love him would delight to-night to greet. In behalf of those of them who are absent I send this message of grateful homage and regard.

"And I am dear Dr. Chambers,

"Very Faithfully yours,

"H. C. POTTER."

The Chairman Continued—

We are fortunate to have the presence of him to whom Dr. Dix refers as his "young friend and brother" the Rev. Richard D. Harlan, who is now the minister of the First Presbyterian Church of New York, the oldest of that honored name in this city ; and he will speak to us on the present occasion.

The Address
Of the Rev. Richard D. Harlan.

FATHERS AND BRETHREN:

AS we are met together to offer our thanksgiving to the Head of the Church for the fifty years' service which this reverend father in God has been permitted to give to one branch of the Catholic Church, and to bring our heartfelt congratulations to him upon the advent of this jubilee year, I think it is fitting that we should at the same time be reminded of the great age of that historic church of which he is so honored a minister.

I regret exceedingly that Dr. Dix is not present this evening. Were he here, I know that he would join with me, as the representatives of our respective denominations, in admitting that, in comparison with the Reformed Church on Manhattan Island, we Episcopalians and Presbyterians are all of us schismatics. The facts are these: the sturdy Dutch forefathers planted their first, this Collegiate Church, within the town of New Amsterdam in the year of Our Lord 1628; old Trinity was not founded until sixty-six years afterward, in 1696, while the church of which I have the honor to be the minister, is by eighty-three years the junior of the Collegiate Church, not being organized until 1711. So that we may as well frankly admit to you, our brethren of the Dutch Church, that you are the Established Church of New York, while Dr. Dix and I, together with all our colleagues of the Presbyterian and Episcopal order, are dissenters. Therefore, in bringing our congratulations to this reverend bishop of so ancient a church, fairly hoary with age for our youthful republic, we feel (and I speak for Dr. Dix as well as myself), as if we ought to offer some kind of an apology for this high-handed act of what we Churchmen know as territorial schism. However, I am sure that our reverend father will not ask for such an apology; for he knows well that there is room and to spare, for all of us, each to do our own God-given and peculiar work in this many sided population. If I may be permitted to use a phrase which is no longer correct or descriptive, I would say that we aim not to make Dutchmen, nor Episcopalians, nor even Presbyterians, but to make Christians, to enroll at our respective recruiting stations, volunteers for life-long service as soldiers of Jesus Christ. In a spirit of generous emulation which does not run into petty sectarian rivalry, in a spirit of mutual and proper preference each for his own church, which does not exalt or rather contract itself into exclusiveness, we labor side by side in this great metropolis, which so throbs with life and teems with problems. We feel the bondage of the same sin; we are heralds of the same glad tidings of God's love to men; we are children of the one common

Father: we love and serve the one Great Redeemer; we cling to the same cross; we point the weary feet of men to the same Heavenly Father's house. I once heard an aged saint say that we Christians are very much like the spokes of a wheel, the nearer we get to the centre the nearer we come to one another. And I think it is one of the jubilant signs of the times, a sign which is most vividly recalled to us on such an occasion as this, with its many catholic features, to observe the way in which all who profess and call themselves Christians are hastening toward the day when we shall all live together in the unity of the Spirit, in the bond of peace, and in righteousness of life.

And as I am on the edge of this burning question which throbs at the heart of all Christendom, one fact occurs to me which it gives me peculiar pleasure as a minister of the Presbyterian order, to give utterance to, an incident which I believe has not yet been noticed, and which for the very reason that it has been forgotten or lost sight of as a matter of no vital importance (and it certainly is not remembered with any unchristian or jealous feeling on the part of the church that I represent), shows how low the walls are between us and how we pass and re-pass without friction. I refer to the fact that Dr. Vermilye was reared as a Presbyterian and was first ordained as a minister of that body; but early in his career, finding that he could serve his Divine Master better in the communion of the Reformed Church, transferred his membership to you and was enrolled as a minister of the Classis of Albany. As a matter of history I understand that he is the oldest living licentiate of the New York Presbytery. We reared and trained him for you, and these fifty years of faithful service are a sufficient proof of the soundness and efficient thoroughness of that training. Therefore we Presbyterians claim a peculiar right to participate in these ceremonies, and we take a peculiar pleasure in bringing our congratulations upon this auspicious semi-centennial occasion.

I need not refer at length to Dr. Vermilye's services in the Board of Trustees of the Leake and Watts Orphan

House; that has been already touched upon by my colleague Dr. Dix. For three and a half years during my ministry in New York, by reason of my official association with the Senior Minister of the Collegiate Church in the management of that beautiful charity, I have had the privilege of knowing Dr. Vermilye personally ; and very vivid to the memory will always be the picture of him as he participated in the meetings of the Board or was an interested spectator of the children's performances at the annual commencements at the Orphan House—his face beaming with placid benignity, writ in large fair characters in every lineament of his countenance, his very presence a benediction. May that presence remain with us and with you, many years : and may the Lord lift up the light of His countenance upon him, and give him His everlasting peace, until that day when he shall be gathered as a full shock of corn into the heavenly garner.

The Chairman then said :—Before we sing, as marked on the programme, I will call the attention of the congregation to the beautiful basket of flowers on my right hand, which comes from the trustees and officers and children of the Leake, and Watts Orphan House, in testimony of their respect and affection for one who has served them so long and so faithfully.

The MAGNIFICAT IN A. (J. Stainer) was then sung, after which the Chairman said : I have the pleasure of introducing to the audience Hon. ENOCH L. FANCHER, President of The American Bible Society, who on this occasion will represent not only that great national institution, of which he is the honored President, but that eminent body of active and enterprising Christians known as the Methodist Episcopal Church.

The Address of the Hon. Enoch L. Fancher.

I ESTEEM it a privilege to be present on this occasion of joyful congratulation to a distinguished servant of the Church, and to bring to him the felicitations of the officers and managers of the American Bible Society.

We certainly must all believe that it is a high distinction to have attained the completion of such service as he has performed for the last fifty years. Now, weighted with honor, surrounded by admiring friends, and blessed with the memories of so long a service as fifty years, he certainly must look back upon his pathway with gratitude to God and with gladness of heart. He occupies a permanent place in the high regard of his church and of this community. His associate pastors and many other Christian ministers and friends, friends in the laity as well, rejoice to honor him and to proffer him their congratulations. Among those rejoicing friends, the officers and managers of the American Bible Society are glad to appear. They do not forget that Dr. Vermilye, before he was called to the sacred ministry, while yet, I believe, a student of law, was a witness to the formation of the American Bible Society in one of the rooms of the City Hall of this City. And since his consecration to the sacred ministry he has been an efficient advocate of its cause ; for a long, long time, a member of its most important Committee, on " Revision," during which time the laborious work was performed of preparing a revised edition of the sacred book ; and since that time he has rendered efficient aid to the Society in the deliberations of its Board of Managers. The records of eternity must be unrolled before it can be known how many, how very many, souls have been lighted by the wisdom of the Divine Word through the instrumentality of the honored guest of this evening. I bring from the American Bible Society its chaplet of acknowledgment and honor, to place lovingly upon the brow of so distinguished a champion of its cause ; and it does not need the partiality of personal acquaintance to convey this wreath with the loftiest encomium for Dr. Vermilye's services as a friend of every good cause in this City, and as a Christian minister his history is perfectly familiar to all of us. His associates of the Collegiate Church, and many Christian brethren both of the clergy and laity, proclaim his praise ; while the record of his fifty years' pastoral work in one of the noblest church organizations in New York adds lustre to his name.

What affectionate interests gather around the commemoration of this event! A saintly minister, a faithful pastor, a popular preacher, and sound theologian, of whose goodness and qualifications his lengthened service and his endeared relations to his church, to the Bible and other benevolent causes, testify, and who has been for so many years recognized as a peer among that brilliant galaxy of Christian ministers of the Reformed Dutch Church of America, receives to-night the acclamations and the plaudits of his brethren and friends as he completes the half century of his blessed work. It is certainly but the performance of a proper, as well as a pleasant duty, to hail him as the successful champion and to lift the acclaim, "Servant of God, well done!"

Several of the temples in which he has ministered stand as bulwarks strong, their spires pointing to the skies: but they are not more conspicuous nor permanent than the undying influence of the work of him whom we are met to honor.

In our busy City, where human lives for a large part are mingled with hopes disappointed and aims unattained, and when the best endeavors are defeated by a thousand mischances, it seems more like a fancied fable than a real fact, that one who while connected with a single church organization has attained the "consummation so devoutly to be wished," as a completion of a half century of efficient work, uninterrupted by any lapse or disappointment; and in contemplating such success we must believe that some native force of character, some peculiar cultivation of temperament, some unusual physical and intellectual endowments, and some singular impartation of divine grace have contributed to the felicitous result.

And how is the coveted grandeur of mere wordly distinctions rebuked and brought into littleness as we contemplate such a useful and well-spent service of fifty years! Such a long term of benevolent usefulness has a vibration far beyond the limits of the church and congregations in which it was rendered, for its widening circles reach the community at large and its influence does not terminate with its end; it rolls on like a tide without an ebb.

I would avoid any officious familiarity toward one of so lofty a position and high attainments as those of Dr. Vermilye, and yet I am constrained for one moment to refer to some incidents relating to his early appearance in the pulpits of the Collegiate Church. About the time that he was called as an associate pastor of the Collegiate Church, I came to the City of New York and entered upon the study of the law. Being a stranger here, I inquired where I might hear the great preachers, I was directed to a church,—the North Dutch Church I think it was called,—situate on the corner of Fulton and William Streets. And going there, I heard sermons, several of them from those masters of pulpit oratory and power, the Rev. Drs. Brownlee and DeWitt. The former preached some sermons in which he assailed the infidel literature of the time, with strong argument and invective: and the latter rolled along like a hero in his triumphal chariot, an adept in theology and pulpit power. Both of those great men were celebrities in their day and were well considered God-anointed kings of thought. And when I heard that an associate pastor had been called to the pulpit of the Collegiate Church, I formed an idea—a mistaken idea it was—that he would fall below the high standard of popularity raised by his predecessors. But when I had heard the new preacher, to whom so many young persons were at that time attracted, I saw that he held no second place in the estimation of his auditors nor in the power of his position as a colleague and peer among princes of the pulpit. If his predecessors were a Paul in argument and a Cephas in power, he seemed to be an Apollos of finished utterance, where every delicacy of speech and grace of harmony was made impressive by a voice of silver tone and a countenance that beamed like a benediction

There hung against the upper ceiling high over the pulpit, an escutcheon with the device "Dando Conservat," which to my youthful sense at first seemed very paradoxical, for I thought how can one save by giving? The device, no doubt, had reference to the benevolent donor of property to the church; and it seems to me it is quite appropriate to borrow its sentiment for this occasion.

Here present with us is one who has for fifty years given his time, his talents, his pastoral and benevolent labor, and, so to speak, his all, for the advancement of the Bible cause and of every other good cause, and for the further-ance of the glorious gospel of the Blessed God. And must we not say "conservat," "He saves"? Saves the happy memories of many useful years, the serene satisfaction of labors well bestowed, the admiring appreciation of cordial friends, and the blissful hope of future good, a hope all intense and bright with the forevisions of the blessed Land. No life has a grander history than that of such a Christian minister: he has been teacher, consoler and bene-factor. The excellency of dignity and the excellency of honor pertain to him; he has feared God and known no other fear, and by precept and example has allured to brighter worlds and leads the way.

Before I take my seat, as Dr. Chambers has said, I rep-resent the Methodist Episcopal Church as well as the American Bible Society, I desire to offer a word of criti-cism on something that fell from the lips of our esteemed friend, Mr. Harlan. The first Church that was organized in this country was the Methodist Episcopal Church: and that is *the* established church, if you must go back to the history of organization to find a definition of that word. *

---

* The playful reference of Judge Fancher was to the fact that the other churches mentioned had been organized in the Colonial period, whereas the M. E. Church had its formal beginning just after the States became a nation.

He says: "It is not meant by this that other churches did not *exist* here—the Dutch Church had a long antecedent existence. Stevens, Vol. 1, p. 269, says in his History: American Methodism 'virtually became independent at the breaking-out of the' (Revolutionary) 'war, and the Constitution which organized it into the Methodist Episcopal Church was to be adopted in about one year after the treaty of peace with Great Britain, and to precede the adoption of the Federal Consti-tution by about five years. The new church was to be the first religious body of the country which should recognize in its organic law, by a solemn declaration of

The Chairman then said : Before announcing the last speaker, I wish to relate an incident suggested by something that Judge Fancher has remarked. About five and twenty years ago I was called to see a man in middle life who was attacked with a mortal disease. He was not a confessed disciple of Christ, and in conversation I remember to have asked him if he had any doubts about the Christian religion or any scruples respecting the divine origin of the Bible. The answer was this :—"I had them once but on a certain occasion I heard a sermon form Dr. Vermilye on the purity of the Bible, and I have never had a doubt since." This sermon was one of a series delivered by distinguished ministers of our City at the request of the American Bible Society in commemoration of their Jubilee, which occurred in 1866, and the testimony thus given is I think indubitable and clear, to the convincing force and persuasiveness of the discourse then delivered.

We shall now be addressed by Dr. MERRILL E. GATES, the President of Rutgers College, who will come to us not only as representing that venerable literary institution of which he is the head, but as speaking for the general interests of sound learning and a liberal education, of which my venerable colleague was always an earnest friend and advocate.

Address of President Gates.

IT is with especial pleasure that I bring from Rutgers College, where the life-tide of strong young manhood flows full and deep, a message of congratulation to the venerable scholar whose ripe, old age we honor to-night, since 1849 a trustee of that College, and for some years now, the senior member of its Board of Trustees.

I have often felt, my friends, and never more deeply than to-night, that we need in our church-life a form of religious festival for Christian old age, that shall be the counterpart of the joyous *christening* we give our children. To complete the connected view of our " covenant theology," as it works itself out in the history of a Christian life on the earth, the Church needs some grateful recognition of the ripened graces and consummated blessings of a serene Chris-

its Articles of Religion, the *new Republic;* the first to pay homage, in the persons of its chief representatives, its first bishops, to the Supreme Magistracy.'"

tian old age. And it might be well at times to make this recognition as joyous and as public as is the christening. Why should all public garnering of the rich lessons from a long Christian life, be confined to those funeral occasions when the perception of the blessings God has given in such a life. is dimmed and chastened by the sense of bereavement and loss?

The wealth of hopes that centre about the young life, as it is brought into God's house for baptism, and by the parents' faith has its infant feet set in the pathway of covenanted mercies, are in part hopes for this temporal life, and in part hopes that take hold on eternity. Often in God's dealing with us, the young life is withdrawn into a higher life, before these hopes for usefulness on earth have reached fruition. With that rich prodigality of life that marks its initial stages everywhere, many of the fairest spring blossoms fall before the fruit is set.

But when the life on this earth is rounded out to generous completion; when the dangers that beset childhood, the temptations that surround youth, the burdens that are laid on mature manhood, and the storms and trials that beset the way through all the allotted three score years and ten, are passed, and safely and triumphantly passed; when the active years have been filled with usefulness, with broad scholarly interests and practical Christian helpfulness; when the voyage of life has brought one to the serene, placid expanse of an evening-lake, protected from storms, and lighted up and glorified by the full beams from a western sky that opens into Heaven; when a Christian life thus blessed has securely reached an anniversary as significant as is the one we commemorate to-night, we do well to observe the day with especial joy and Christian cheerfulness. And our Dutch Church, always tenderly human-hearted in its recognition of the individual life of the believer, starting in its favorite catechism with the individual believer's "only comfort in life and death," and in its liturgy and in its doctrines pulsing with the heart-beats of a human life touched by the divine life of Christ, is led most naturally to come to God's house to-night, to render grateful recognition to a Father Whose hand has guided, and Whose love has blessed this long and honorable life.

It is a spirit too circumspect and over-fearful that breathes in the shrewd warning "call no man happy until death is passed." For Christians, children of a King Who giveth grace and strength, there is a fuller confidence, a more rationally hopeful view of life. While we reverently acknowledge that all the strength and grace which upholds men among temptations from within and without, is given from God, yet we have such entire confidence in his promises that we dare believe that His grace will not fail one who in youth accepted its "covenanted securities," who has worked in its strength through many years, and who now "leans upon the arm of his Beloved," as the vital forces of the body fail, and leave the life of the soul more engrossingly real. Such an one as our venerated friend, we dare to pronounce *most happy*, even before the last chapter of his earthly life is written. For death cannot touch those treasures of experience and faith that the aged Christian has laid up, there where his heart is!

And there is a precious experience of Christian faith which we do well to cherish and rely upon, which reminds us all, even in the careless years of youth and the hurrying years of active burden-bearing in later life, that an Eternal Omnipotent Energy is pledged to carry forward the work of grace in every life that is "born of God, by faith in the Lord Jesus Christ." Like the swell of the eternal sea-voice in the night-silences to all dwellers on the shore, there rolls in upon us again and again the assuring voice of Him whose word cannot be broken, "This is the will of God, even your sanctification." And what can defeat His holy will?

With full assurance, then, we call our friend most happy, μακάριος, *blessed*, whatever else life may have in store for him.

The services were closed with the Doxology, after which a benediction was pronounced by the Rev. Roderick Terry, D.D., Pastor of the South Reformed Church.

THE following appropriate and touching discourse, suggested by the Commemorative Service, was delivered by Doctor Coe in the Church at Fifth Avenue and Forty-eighth Street, on Sunday morning, November 10, 1889, and is here appended by direction of the Consistory.

On Growing Old.

A SERMON BY THE REV. EDWARD B. COE, D.D.

It shall come to pass that at evening time there shall be light.—ZECHARIAH xiv., 7.

MANY of you were doubtless present at the service which was held in this place a few evenings since, to celebrate the fiftieth anniversary of the installation of our beloved and honored senior Pastor. It was certainly fitting that an event so unusual as the accomplishment of a pastorate of fifty years' duration in the service of the same church and of a career of over sixty years in the ministry of the Gospel should receive this public and grateful recognition. The service was, I think, worthy of the occasion. It was a peculiar pleasure to us who worship here thus to express our respect and affection for the dear and venerable man, whose benignant and beautiful presence we always love to see among us. The words that were spoken by those who represented other branches of the Church and important institutions of religion and philanthropy were a hearty and well merited tribute to one of so catholic a spirit and of such wide and varied usefulness. And a still more impressive and memorable tribute was paid to him by the presence of so large and distinguished a company, representing our own denomination and many others, representing various institutions and organizations, and the Christian public of this and other cities, uniting in a demonstration of respect and esteem for one whose long life has been spent in the service of God and of his fellow-men. It was a noble and in all respects a suitable ovation to our honored Father and Friend.

It may have caught the attention of some of those who were then present that the words which I have read as the text for this morning were quoted in two of the addresses that were made on that occasion: " At evening time there shall be light." They seem to be peculiarly appropriate to a serene Christian old age, like that of which we then had before us so striking and so charming an example. And now it is of such an old age and the way to attain it, that I want to speak this morning, and I therefore recall again to your minds these ancient words which are so beautifully descriptive of it.

It is true that in the connection in which they are found they have nothing to do with old age. They form part of a highly poetic and somewhat obscure prophecy of the final deliverance and triumph of the Church of God. The time will come, the prophet says, when the people of God shall no longer be shut up in Jerusalem, but the Mount of Olives shall be cleft in twain, half of it shall be removed toward the north and half toward the south, and through it shall be opened " a very great valley " by which they shall go forth to the ends of the earth; two perpetual streams of living water shall flow forth from the Holy City toward the east and the west ; the whole land shall be leveled that the mountain of the Lord's house may be exalted ; and the Lord shall be king over all the earth. And the day when all this shall come to pass shall be no ordinary day. " The light shall not be with brightness and with gloom "—with the ordinary succession of morning and evening ; but " the day shall be *one* "—unique in the history of the world; " which is known unto the Lord," and to Him alone; " not day and not night," but something different from either; "and it shall come to pass that at evening time," when in the usual course of nature darkness should set in, " there shall be light." In this ornate and splendid imagery the prophet portrays the ultimate triumph of Messiah's Kingdom, for which, like him, we still hope and wait. But this last trait of his inspired description has been many times fulfilled in the personal experience of God's people, as well as in the history of the Church. It has been light at eventide. At the moment when it seemed as if overwhelming disaster was imminent, and the end of all things was near at hand, there has suddenly come unexpected deliverance. So it was with Abraham, when the altar was built, and the fire laid, and the knife lifted to slay his son. Not till then did God provide the lamb for a burnt-offering. So it was with his descendants in the land of their oppression, deliverance coming only when the utmost extremity of suffering had been reached, so that the saying became a proverb, "When the straw fails then comes Moses." So when the Lord knew that Lazarus whom He loved was sick, He abode still for two days in the place where He was and spent two days more on the journey to Bethany, that by a transcendent and conclusive display of His divine power He might the more signally exhibit the glory of God. And so when Peter lay in prison, and prayer was unceasingly made to God for him, it was not till the night preceding the day appointed for his execution that the iron gate opened before him of its own accord, and he was given back to the Church which so urgently needed him. And so it has been a thousand times in the history of the Church and in the personal lives of those who compose it. When hope has almost died out, deliverance has come. When the enemies of the faith have seemed about to triumph, they have been overthrown. When some great calamity has been impending, it has been averted. Prayer has been answered when it seemed as if it could not be answered, and when the night was closing in, in starless gloom, at evening time there has been light. Man's extremity has been God's opportunity, and even if it is not strictly true, either in the physical or in the spiritual world, that the darkest hour is that which immediately precedes the dawn, it is certainly true that it is often God's way sorely to test the faith and patience of his people before he interposes for their relief. And we may well pause upon this fact long enough to gather up the lessons of meek endurance and of unfaltering trust, which spring directly from the prophet's words. It is never too late for

God to exhibit His pity and His power in answer to prayer, and it is as easy for Him to cause the light to shine out again from the gathering darkness, as it is to hold the sun suspended on His word in the noonday sky.

But if this is the primary meaning of the passage, it receives no violence from that natural impulse which leads us to apply it to what we so often call the evening of life when the shadows lengthen along our path, and the hour draws near when our hands must be folded and our eyes closed for the last sleep. No man can tell, of course, how long his life is to be, or when or how it is to end. It may be like a day in June, when the sun lingers long above the horizon and seems reluctant to disappear behind those gates of amethyst and gold, which finally hide him from our sight; when a rich and mellow and tranquil light fills all the air, and one can hardly tell when the invisible line is crossed which divides day from night. And it may be like a December day, which is gone almost before we realize that it is here, when the sun is extinguished before it reaches the meridian, or sets in cold and stormy clouds. There may be no long and luminous twilight, but the night comes sharply down before the work of the day is finished. And then there are lives so brief that we cannot compare them to a *day* at all, with its slow approach, its steady and even march of hours, and its gradual and orderly close. They are rather like a strain of exquisite music, or like the flash of a bird's wing across the azure. They pass, and we awake, and lo! it was a dream! So what the length of our life shall be we cannot tell. To some of us old age has already come. We are forced to confess it. The keepers of the house have already begun to tremble, and the strong men to bow themselves; the grinders have almost ceased because they be few, and those that look out of the windows are darkened; the daughters of music have been brought low, the almond tree is in blossom, and the grasshopper is a burden, and desire has failed, and our long home (or rather our eternal house) is not far off. By signs that cannot be mistaken, old age has marked us for its own. There are others, who feel themselves to be rapidly approaching that last chapter of their earthly history; and others still who are just opening the mysterious book of life, and who find its pages throbbing with an intense and passionate interest. How far God will suffer us to read on before He closes the volume for us, it is impossible to say. But whether we realize that we are actually growing old, or only know that it is possible that we too may one day be aged men or women, it is to all of us a matter of importance to consider how we may grow old beautifully.

For such a thing there certainly is, as a beautiful old age. The evening of life is sometimes the loveliest and most blessed part of life—when the heat and flurry of youth is over, when the strain and stress of middle life is past, and like a ship that has made its voyage successfully, one drops anchor at last in the safe and sheltered harbor. Then the violence of passion is subdued, the burden of care and responsibility and labor is left to others who are younger, the eager striving for that which is beyond gives place to the quiet enjoyment of that which is already gained, the strained and care-worn look vanishes from the face, which now shines with a soft and tranquil light, and the voice which was once imperious and commanding is subdued to sweeter tones of sympathy and love. The mind and heart are both at peace—the one from its restless questionings and the other from its eager ambitions. The discipline of sorrow has borne its fruit in a temper of humble and trustful submission to a higher will, and a broader and deeper charity has come with its heavenly grace upon the positive and vehement spirit. That is certainly a beautiful old age, and there are none of us, probably, who have not seen examples of it which have exerted a blessed and imperishable influence upon us. If they have passed from our homes to the home above, the memory of them is among our most precious possessions. If they still tarry with us, we bless God for them, and pray that He will spare, as long as may be, to us and to our children, their gentle and gracious presence.

But such is not always the character of old age. One sometimes grows narrower as he grows older—more stern, exacting, uncharitable, selfish. The frank generosity of youth is changed to a grasping and miserly temper. Misfortune and disappointment embitter instead of chastening the spirit. The decay of bodily vigor produces restlessness and discontent. One is peevish and complaining and suspicious and jealous. The habit of command is not willingly laid aside, though the judgment may have lost its earlier vigor. There is not "light at eventide," but only a dull and darkening sky. And such a wearing away of life is sad to see. There are cases in which we cannot wonder at it. The wonder is rather that it is not more frequent. It would seem to be natural that long years of trial, and the knowledge that all must soon be over, would depress the mind and sour the temper and make old age a time of gloom. And the fact that it is so often *not* that, but a time of serenity and cheerfulness, of "sweetness and light," seems to imply that there is a secret of growing old beautifully, which is well worth our while to discover, if we can.

I think it is found, in the first place, in frankly accepting old age when it comes. I freely grant that this is not easy. It is hard to admit that one's work in the world is nearly done. It is hard to resign to others the places of honor and of influence that one has held for many years. It is hard to accept authority where one has long been used to the exercise of it, and to see younger men managing affairs that we have long been accustomed to direct. It is not pleasant to realize that the world can get along without us, and that those whom we have perhaps trained to their work are now more competent to carry it on than we are ourselves. It is not easy to resign the admiration and deference which were shown to us when we were in the full vigor of life, or agreeable to fancy that we can detect a certain element of toleration even in the respectful and affectionate treatment which we still receive. And, of course, it is not pleasant to feel the consciousness of failing powers of body or mind, to see the beautiful bloom of youth fading from the face, and to discover that the body which has so long been our servant no longer promptly obeys the still vigorous will. There are some things connected with the coming on of old age which no one can perceive without a feeling of sadness.

But, on the other hand, it is of no use to deny any fact —least of all, the fact that we are growing old. We cannot alter or even conceal it, and it is worse than in vain to struggle against it. There are few things sadder, because more un-natural, than for one to try to keep up the illusion of youth, when youth has long since been left behind—to pretend to be standing on the hill-tops of life, when one is already far down its western slope. The light that brightens the even-ing time is not that of gaudy and sputtering tapers or even that of the brilliant electric arc. Neither of these can be for a moment mistaken for the soft radiance of the setting sun. It only makes the closing years of life harder to bear and robs them of their peculiar charm, to fight against the order of nature or to murmur and fret because the tide of time is bearing us on. One must, first of all, be on good terms with old age, if he hopes to make it beautiful.

And then it is certainly a great mistake to suppose that the work of life is done when one has grown old. Its nature is changed, but it is not finished. The work of life is never done till life itself is ended. It was only a few days since that an aged man said to me—a man who, with his wife, is not only far advanced in years, but has lately been passing through an experience of great distress: " I sometimes wonder why God spares us any longer." I replied, " I know perfectly well why He spares you. There is no mys-tery about that. The mystery is only in the suffering that He has seen fit to send upon you. But He keeps you here for the sake of the rest of us; to give us an example of pa-tience and cheerfulness and unwavering Christian faith." And every one who knows him would, I am sure, have said just the same thing. I often wish that those who feel that their work is ended, because they are now able to do so little, could only realize how much they are doing by simply being what they are. What a glory and grace would pass from our life if it were not for the benignant light which shines upon it from their lovely and serene old age! It is even doubtful whether, in the time of their fullest vigor and activity, they were able to do so much as they are now doing for the Master and for their fellow-men.

And so of the honor and affection which old age excites in all but the coarsest and most vulgar minds. It is not, of course, precisely the same which manly strength and womanly beauty were wont to command in earlier years. But there is less of selfishness in it, and more of deep and genuine homage. It may be confined to a narrower circle, but it is none the less precious for that. The silent and loving devotion of the young to the old, which adorns so many Christian homes, is of far greater value than the applause of admiring assemblies or the crude stare of gaping crowds.

There are thus, as I am sure you will all admit, some compensations in growing old, and the point that I am urging is, that it is well for those of us who have reached, or are nearing, that period of life, to take the comfort of thoughts like these; to count up their gains instead of fretting at their losses; and not to make the limitations, of which they are becoming conscious, harder to bear by struggling against them. One secret of a beautiful old age is the frank acceptance of it.

Another is found in that to which I have just alluded —the considerate and honoring love of those among whom it is spent. It is, of course, of no use to preach about this to elderly people. They know more about it than I can tell them. But it *is* worth while to remind those who are young, from the little children upward, how largely it depends on them to make bright and tranquil the evening of life for those whose sun is near its setting. I should not like to say that disrespect to the aged is a distinctive trait of American character, for that would be drawing up a harsh indictment against an entire people. But one can hardly deny that there is often shown by

our jaunty and self-satisfied young men and young women a contemptuous disregard of the opinions, the comfort
and the rights of those who are old, which is a blot on
our manners and is deserving of instant and stern rebuke.
A more unmistakable sign of native coarseness and selfishness can scarcely be conceived, and it disgraces forever
any one who displays it. And so, on the other hand,
hardly anything is more beautiful than the thoughtful and
affectionate courtesy and devotion which it is often in the
power of the young to show toward the aged. It has its
immediate reward in the grace which it adds to old age
itself, and it is sure to be among the things which it will
be most sweet to remember, when those to whom it has
been offered have passed away. That must be a sour and
crabbed nature which does not respond to it, as an aged
tree responds in every shimmering leaf to the warming
touch of the summer sun. If there are any of us to whom
it is still permitted to render such loving ministries to
those on whose heads God has set the silver crown of
years, let us never forget that the light which cheers the
evening of life is partly that which is reflected from the
loving hearts and faces of those on whom the morning sun
is shining still.

And yet it is not, after all, so much an outward as an
inward light which makes old age serene and beautiful.
And that must come in great measure through the medium
of memory. Old age lives, largely, in the past. Not
wholly in the past, if it is to retain its fresh and vigorous
life. One of the things which contribute most to this, is
to keep in touch (as the phrase now is) with the actual
on-going life of the world. If it is possible to cling too
long to the outward signs of youth, it is possible also to re-
tire too soon and too completely from all knowledge of and
all interest in the things in which one can no longer bear
an active part. This is the way to grow old with needless
rapidity and to bury one's self before one is dead. It is
charming to see in an aged person a living and animated
interest in that which is taking place around him and in

which others are actively concerned. It shows a perennial youthfulness of spirit, which is not to be confounded with a fictitious youthfulness of manner or of dress.

But, after all, memory plays a large rôle in the life of one who has come to old age. And hence it is that if any man's old age—yours and mine, for example—is to be serene and happy, he must be able to look back upon a life that has been on the whole well spent. It is not necessary that it should have been free from sorrow. Few long lives are so, and it is not the memory of even great sorrows which brings sadness and gloom into the evening of life. God kindly permits the wounds of the heart to heal with time, as He hides the gashes and fissures that His storms and earthquakes make in the surface of the fields with a thick and delicate net-work of grasses and flowers. Nor is it necessary that one should be able to recall triumphant successes and heroic exploits, though such memories undoubtedly gladden and glorify the declining days of one who is able to look back upon them. But to feel that one's life has been altogether a failure, that he has wasted his strength, his time, his opportunity, that he has lived in a wholly selfish and sordid way and has done little or nothing for God or man—that is to sit down at eventide with the light that is in him as darkness itself. There are many motives by which we are prompted to right and earnest living. That which I now urge is one of the lowest. But it is at least worth while to remember, that however it may be with the world to come, there is prepared for many men a judgment-day in the present world, and they themselves are to act as judges. It is that period of life, when, having finished their work, they look back upon it as memory brings it before their view. And few things can be sadder than to see, when it cannot be altered, that it has all been in vain. If you want your last days to be beautiful, make the present day beautiful. If you desire to be able to look back over your life with any degree of satisfaction, do your work well as you go along. Tears shed by and by will not wash out failures made now. When you are old and gray-headed you cannot undo what you are doing now. A life devoted to the service of God and to the service of your fellow-men out of love to God, is the only kind of life which you will rejoice to recall, when you stand among the evening shadows. Not what you have gained or what you have enjoyed, but what you have done or have not done will make that hour bright or dark.

And yet in all this there would be little comfort for most of us, if it were not for one other thing. Who of us has lived, or is now living, such a life that he can look back upon it with much satisfaction? It may not be an absolute failure. It may not be wholly selfish or worldly. We have honestly desired, and honestly tried, to do our duty to God and to our fellow-men. But how sadly we have come short of our duty! How little we have accomplished! Might we not almost as well have made no effort? Oh, that we could live our lives over again! There is little to cheer us, little to brighten our eventide, in the memory of opportunities neglected, of duties left undone, of privileges unused, of a high ideal so miserably missed. That is surely a very common feeling among even the best of men, as they look backward over their earthly lives. And so I must add that the evening of life will be full of self-reproach and bitter humiliation, if one has no hope in the forgiving mercy and grace of God. It will not perhaps seem to you a fanciful figure, if I say that the light of memory is very much like that of the electric point. It is very brilliant and very penetrating, but it is ill-diffused. It brings out certain objects with startling distinctness, but it leaves others in profoundest shadow. It has no warmth or glow whatever, and it dazzles you at one moment and the next moment leaves you in darkness. So it is with memory. Better, almost, no light at all than its flashing and misleading ray! No; the light that fills the evening of life with a soft and mellow glory is that sense of God's love in the believing soul, which enables one to recall even the failures and sins of the past without dismay, in the assurance that they are covered by that infinite grace which was manifested in Jesus Christ. There is nothing else—no outward circumstance of love or of honor, no memory of brave or heroic deeds—which can illumine the soul, as it draws near the end of its mortal career, like this tranquilizing and uplifting faith. Men may be calm and cheerful without it, dismissing from their minds whatever disturbs their repose, and shutting their eyes to facts which it is not agreeable to face ; but the peace which passes the world's understanding, and which the world can neither give nor take away, belongs only to one whose soul rests upon the promises of God, who believes that his errors and sins are forgiven him for the sake of Christ's sufferings and death, and who knows himself to be safe in the strong arms of that divine, redeeming love. If you want to know the secret of the beautiful serenity which you have sometimes seen on the face of the aged Christian, *that is it*. He knows the love of Christ which passeth knowledge.

There is but one thing more ; what else can there be except the expectation of the life to come? The earthly life is still real and dear, but it is fading away, as the shores of one's native land sink slowly out of sight as his ship forges onward into the open sea. But one who knows himself to be God's child, enfolded in the Father's love, is never out of sight of land. He can discern before him a fairer country, even an heavenly, which is not very far off, and to which he is drawing nearer every day. It has been growing more real to him year by year, as those whom he has loved have gone thither before him, until on its silent and shining shore there are many now who await his coming. Sometimes · it seems as if the beauty that is on his face were reflected from that which our dimmer eyes cannot perceive; as if the light which brightens the close of his earthly day shone on him out of the open and waiting heavens, whose golden threshold his feet have almost touched. However it be, we know that it is the vision of the city above which consoles and inspires him as he moves onward toward it, and by and by it will indeed be " light about him," when he passes out of the earthly shadows into the immortal day.

My friends, I do not wish to exaggerate anything, but I

simply say that there is not now, and never has been, a power on earth which could give to old age such a heavenly beauty as this, but the gospel of Christ. If you and I accept it and live by it, it will matter very little where, or when, or how we may end our days; to us also the words of the promise will be fulfilled, that "at evening time there shall be light." May God grant it to us all!

THE CORPORATION IN 1839.

MINISTERS.

The Rev. JOHN KNOX, D.D.
The Rev. WILLIAM CRAIG BROWNLEE, D.D.
The Rev. THOMAS DE WITT, D.D.

ELDERS.	DEACONS.
DAVID BOARD,	THEOPHILUS ANTHONY,
HENRY HAVENS,	JOHN I. BROWER,
CORNELIUS HEYER,	THOMAS GRAHAM,
WILLIAM G. JONES,	CHARLES J. JOHNSON,
JOHN NEILSON,	JAMES V. H. LAWRENCE,
SAMUEL PENNY,	CALEB F. LINDSLEY,
ISAAC SEBRING,	JAMES MEYERS,
CORNELIUS R. SUYDAM,	ADRIAN H. MULLER,
VALENTINE VANDEWATER,	JAMES PHYFE,
ABRAHAM VAN NEST,	JOHN T. RUSHER,
JAMES WARD,	JAMES SIMMONS,
NOAH WETMORE,	HIRAM H. VAN VLIET.

OFFICERS.

CORNELIUS BOGERT, *Clerk.*
ISAAC YOUNG, *Treasurer,*

Office, 192 Broadway.

Of the foregoing there are at present only two survivors, Mr. James Simmons, now of Paterson, New Jersey, and Mr. James Meyers, now of Newburg, N. Y.

THE CORPORATION IN 1889.

MINISTERS.

The Rev. THOMAS E. VERMILYE, D.D., LL.D.

The Rev. TALBOT W. CHAMBERS, D.D., LL.D.

The Rev. EDWARD B. COE, D.D.

ELDERS.	DEACONS.
HENRY W. BOOKSTAVER,	GERARD BEEKMAN,
ROBERT BUCK,	WILLIAM L. BROWER,
JOHN S. BUSSING,	WILLIAM C. GIFFING,
PETER DONALD,	WILLIAM P. GLENNEY,
JOHN GRAHAM,	FRANCIS T. LAIMBEER,
FREDERIC R. HUTTON,	FRANCIS T. L. LANE,
LEWIS JOHNSTON,	CHARLES STEWART PHILLIPS,
FREDERICK T. LOCKE,	CHARLES A. RUNK,
EBENEZER MONROE,	CHARLES H. STITT,
RALPH N. PERLEE,	CUMMINGS H. TUCKER, Jr.,
HENRY TALMAGE,	JOSEPH WALKER, Jr.,
CHARLES H. WOODRUFF,	FREDERICK F. WOODWARD.

OFFICERS.

GEORGE S. STITT, *Clerk.*

THEOPHILUS A. BROUWER, *Treasurer,*

Office, 113 Fulton street.

www.ingramcontent.com/pod-product-compliance
Lightning Source LLC
Chambersburg PA
CBHW031750090426
42739CB00008B/957